CHARGED WITH
DRUG POSSESSION
IN TEXAS?

Protect Your Rights, Reclaim Your
Freedom And Go Clean!

MARK DIAZ & JESSICA EBBS

Jacobs & Whitehall
73-03 Bell Blvd, #10
Oakland Gardens, NY 11364
www.jacobsandwhitehall.com

Ordering Information:

Quantity sales. Special discounts are available on quantity purchases by corporations, associations, and others. For details, contact the publisher at the address above.

Orders by U.S. trade bookstores and wholesalers. Please contact Jacobs & Whitehall: Tel: (888) 991-2766 or visit www.jacobsandwhitehall.com.

Printed in the United States of America

Published in 2021

ISBN: 978-1-951149-68-0

PREFACE

Our primary practice area is in Galveston County, Texas. While we regularly handle cases in Harris County, Brazoria County and others; our viewpoint mainly comes from cases in Galveston County. Additionally, we focus on criminal defense of felonies and misdemeanors, most of the information in this book does not apply to Class C Misdemeanors.

While we also handle Federal Criminal Defense, this short booklet deals only with Defense of cases in State/County Court and not Federal cases. While the basic principles of the jury trial, rights, consequences, and role of the Attorney may be similar; punishment and plea bargaining are completely different.

Of course, with all the information available on the internet today, most of the information here in our little publication can be found browsing the internet. This is meant to be a helpful quick read to answer simple questions and help start the process if you have found yourself in the unfortunate position of facing criminal charges. It also gives some insight into the way we try to interact with our clients.

DEDICATION

As always, we would like to dedicate this book to our past, present, and future clients.

Additionally, to our support staff, Shealei Gibbs and Karina Russell.

Lastly, our office mate, RA Apffel, who will turn 91 this October and is still down in the trenches fighting the good fight on a daily basis.

DISCLAIMER

This publication is intended to be used for educational purposes only. No legal advice is being given, and no attorney-client relationship is intended to be created by reading this material. The author assumes no liability for any errors or omissions or for how this book or its contents are used or interpreted, or for any consequences resulting directly or indirectly from the use of this book. For legal or any other advice, please consult an experienced attorney or the appropriate expert, who is aware of the specific facts of your case and is knowledgeable in the law in your jurisdiction.

Mark Diaz & Associates
719 59th St
Galveston, TX 77551
(409) 515-6170
www.texascriminaljustice.com

TESTIMONIALS

"*Mark Diaz and Jessica Ebbs are excellent attorneys. They represented my girlfriend's case and stood by our sides through it all and still to this day are here for us. I highly recommend them to anyone in need of an attorney. They are very hardworking honest and caring individuals who will do anything they can to have the best outcome for you. We knew our future was in good hands and never had to be worried. And also a big thanks to Shealei for everything. Thanks again for everything you all have done for us and the time.*"

– Kyle Chatterton

****

"*Mark Diaz and his team exceeded our expectations and got all charges dropped. Jessica was always there when we needed her and was extremely compassionate and understanding of our family's situation. If we could give this law firm 10 stars we would. We will be recommending them to everyone we know that finds themselves in need of a criminal defense attorney. They are amazing and we are so grateful someone recommended them to us.*"

– Kathy Rife

****

"*Highly, highly recommend anyone who has found themself in a tough situation and don't want something lingering over them for the rest of their lives to give Mark*

Diaz a call. Jessica took a case for me and did a phenomenal job, it's amazing how much she pays attention to detail and goes through every single thing with a fine-toothed comb. I am so thankful for their whole team and especially Jessica for taking their time and making sure every piece was in play. For revealing the real story and sometimes helping the average person who just made a mistake. You guys are awesome! I hope I don't have to call you again but if I ever wind up in a bad situation again you will most definitely be the only ones I want to call. Thank you for always doing such a great job!"

– Daniel McClelland

****

"I have hired Mark on a number of occasions. He is very communicative which is important to me in these situations. He is honest and gives you all the information you need to make an informed decision. I highly recommend Mark and use him exclusively when I require these types of services. I have always had great results when using Mark."

– Alva

****

"We were so grateful to have Mark Diaz in our corner when we needed him. We had no experience with the judicial system, and it was a comfort to know that Mark had experience and first-hand knowledge of the judges and prosecutors. It gave us great comfort to know that he was navigating us through this process."

– Anonymous

****

"Thank you Mark and Jessica for everything! I would definitely recommend to anyone in need of an attorney! They are both professional, hardworking, honest, and caring individuals. They were by my side every step of the way. I truly felt cared for and knew my future was in good hands. I am so grateful that they were able to get my case dismissed! Thank you again for all of your time and energy to help better my future!"

– Marissa Sluss

****

"Mr. Diaz has helped me in numerous cases over the years. He is always available and puts in the extra work for his clients. He loves to win."

– Anonymous

****

"Best Lawyer in Galveston County. Highly recommend to everybody in the area."

– Chad Gaston

TABLE OF CONTENTS

ABOUT THE AUTHORS

Mark Diaz has been aggressively defending the rights of Texans for over eighteen years. A 1998 graduate of Thurgood Marshall School of Law who obtained his undergraduate degree from the University of Houston, Mark concentrates his practice solely in the area of criminal defense. He is admitted to practice law in all Texas state courts as well as the federal court in the United States District Court for the Southern District of Texas. Mark is a seasoned trial lawyer who has tried every kind of criminal defense case.

Mark prides himself on his ability to quickly respond to the needs and concerns of his clients.

Jessica Ebbs

Jessica Ebbs was raised and lives in Galveston County. In 2012, Jessica graduated cum laude from Sam Houston State University with a Bachelor of Business Administration in Accounting. After college, she attended South Texas College of Law and later graduated with her law degree.

After completing law school, Jessica started at the Galveston County District Attorney's Office as an Assistant District Attorney. She began her legal career as an ADA and at first, handled solely misdemeanor cases and was responsible for handling a large volume of cases from the beginning to end and in many situations, trying those cases to a jury.

Within her first year at the Galveston County DA's Office, Jessica was promoted as a felony prosecutor to the 122nd Judicial District Court and later, to the 10th Judicial District Court. As a felony prosecutor, Jessica was responsible for handling all levels of felony cases from onset to finish, including felony jury trials.

Being a prosecutor taught Jessica how to relate with victims and prosecute cases, seeking to uphold the Constitution and the laws of the State of Texas. Jessica now continues her pursuit of justice for those accused of crimes by the State of Texas. Having dealt with hundreds of cases as a prosecutor, Jessica has a thorough understanding of how prosecutors think and how they approach the prosecution of a case. Jessica uses this understanding daily to critically analyze cases and hold prosecutors to their tremendous burden of proving the accused guilty, beyond a reasonable doubt.

Who Is This Book For?

This book is for anyone who is dealing with a drug case or who has a family member who is dealing with a drug case. The issue with these types of cases is that they appear to be somewhat simple, but they are not; they are very technical and when you dive into the issues, they become quite complex unless you are skilled in the issue of drug possession. This book is meant to give clarity for new clients and current clients, and to hopefully give them a greater understanding of the legal process when it comes to defending these types of cases.

CHAPTER 1

WHAT ACTUALLY HAPPENS IF A DRUG CASE GOES TO TRIAL?

On average, you can expect your case to last around the one-year mark, from the time you are arrested to the time you formally go to trial. If the case is actually going to trial, what that looks like is case-specific and of course differs for every person and for every case. Generally speaking, most trials take about a week or less. It usually takes about a day to pick a jury. Then, we proceed to the opening statements of both sides.

Following opening statements, the state puts on its case. They go first because it is their burden to prove a person guilty of the offense charged. What this means is that the state has to prove each and every element of the offense as charged and the allegations against you beyond a reasonable doubt as to each and every element. The state then rests and the defense has an opportunity to present evidence. As the defense, we are not required to put on a case or present any evidence at all. In fact, sometimes it is the best strategy not to if we feel that the state hasn't adequately proven its case.

Once both sides have rested, closing arguments will begin from each side. Then, the jury deliberates and decides whether a person is guilty or not guilty. If they find someone not guilty, everything is over. The charges go away, the defendant is acquitted, and we've done our job. If it goes the other way, then we proceed to the punishment phase of the trial. You keep the same jurors and you start a new phase of trial where the jury decides the appropriate punishment for the crime that the person has been found guilty of.

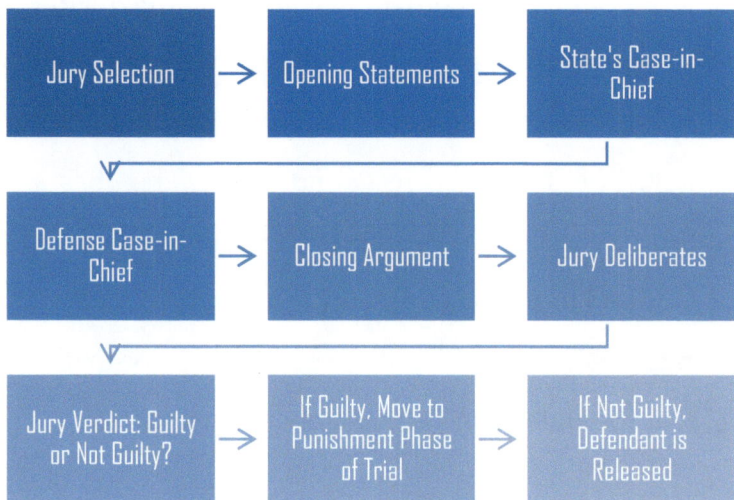

CHAPTER 2

CRITERIA TO DECIDE WHETHER TO TAKE A DRUG CASE TO TRIAL OR TAKE A PLEA OFFER

The first step that we go through in our legal analysis on drug cases is to evaluate the case, which is of course similar to our process in all other cases. We start by asking questions like, "How were the drugs discovered?" "Was that a legal process?" "Was the arrest initiated by first stopping the defendant's vehicle?" "Was that stop legal?"

The next step is examining whether the state can prove possession, which generally speaking means that the accused had care, custody, or control of whatever the substance is they've been charged with. The state has to somehow affirmatively link that substance to the accused.

A good example is if they find a container with drugs in the trunk of a car, but then we find out the car doesn't belong to the defendant. Come to find out, the car was actually his neighbor's and he borrowed it that morning because he had a flat tire. How could he possibly have known that his neighbor had a container with drugs in it in the trunk of the car? More importantly, how can the state present evidence to prove that the defendant knew there was a container of drugs in the trunk of the car? In deciding whether to take a case to trial versus taking a plea, we first to have to do a complete case analysis and determine whether there are legal issues that are worthy of taking to a jury, or perhaps to the judge in suppression hearing where we ask the court to exclude illegally obtained evidence.

If we don't think we can win, then our focus must shift to getting the best possible outcome we can get from the court or the prosecution through a plea bargain. Every case and every client is different. Maybe it is best for the client that we work out a plea deal that reduces the charge and puts the client on a deferred probation, so that they don't end up with a conviction for life. Maybe it is a situation where our client is a 25-to-life but I can get the state to offer me single digits, like a 5. Of course, it is not only my decision; it is a decision that has to be made with the client ultimately deciding what they think the best outcome is based on the options we present them. Throughout the case, we are here to guide clients through the legal analysis and present them with the best options based on their situation, but at the end of the day, it is the client who makes the final decision.

A lot of times, in these cases, there is going to be video available. How did the defendant act on video? Does it corroborate one side or the other? Does it do nothing? How is our client going to be perceived by a jury? That is something we have to consider. It is also important whether the defendant is charged with manufacturing/delivery or whether they are charged with mere possession. Evidence that someone was selling or manufacturing drugs does not generally go over well with a prosecutor or with a jury.

Are Most Drug Related Cases Settled with Plea Deals? Is This (Perhaps Not) Always the Best Option for Clients?

Possession cases are some of the most tried cases in criminal courtrooms. This can largely be attributed to the legal intricacies that most possession cases come down to, including Fourth Amendment search and seizure issues. This is a huge consideration and factor as to whether we should plead the case or go to trial. Client's past convictions can also be a huge factor in deciding how to work the case out.

A lot of clients or potential clients ask us right from the onset what the chances are of a dismissal in their case. This is not a silly question, but unfortunately it isn't one we can ever answer right away. There is no way for us to tell you exactly what it takes and whether a case should plea until we have looked carefully at all the evidence. It is always case specific and client specific. Regardless, we make the client aware of all the risks and benefits that are present with whatever route chosen.

There is sometimes an issue that the state is not willing to offer what we consider to be a good plea bargain for certain cases. For example, if the state is only offering time in the penitentiary, but we think a jury will give our client probation, it may be better to just go to trial. From our perspective, why wouldn't we if a jury will likely give us what we want? It comes down to the individual case, the individual court, and the individual themself. That being said, you have to have an attorney you trust, who is capable of helping you make these decisions.

CHAPTER 3

AT WHAT POINT WILL I HAVE TO ENTER A PLEA OF GUILTY OR NOT GUILTY?

Not every case involves a plea of guilty or not guilty. If we reach a plea agreement between the state and the defense, at that point, you enter a plea of guilty. The only time you ever enter a plea of not guilty would be to go to trial. There are a lot of ways that cases can resolve and they often do without entering a plea of guilty or not guilty. For example, on a misdemeanor possession charge, we often times can work out what we refer to as "terms for a dismissal." In some cases, this may mean the client completes an online drug class and if they do that, then the case gets dismissed. There is never a formal entry of not guilty or guilty. This is case specific and doesn't apply to everyone, but it's an outcome that can be worked out with certain sets of facts and with a good attorney who knows what they are doing and how to navigate the court system where your case is filed.

If I Decide I Want to Enter a Plea of "Not Guilty" and We Go to Trial, What Are the Next Steps?

If you plead not guilty, we secure a trial date with the court. We should have all the evidence that is available to the state at that point. We would want to ensure that and figure out what exactly is going to be presented at trial. Nothing is a surprise; we just sometimes don't know the way the presentation will go. In Texas criminal cases, the state must turn over every piece of evidence they intend to use against you to the defense. That rule doesn't go both ways; from the defense perspective, we are not required to turn over anything. Instead, we can focus on how to best adequately defend you against the state's allegations.

We file all of our pretrial motions and, in drug cases, there can be quite a few. In drug cases, we often file motions to suppress to try to keep out illegally obtained evidence. At that point, we may already have the motion to suppress on file because it is an issue that can be taken up with the court pre-trial.

Once we have a trial setting, we would begin the process of securing witnesses for trial. In some cases, we may also need to begin securing expert witnesses as well. Because as you can imagine, expert witnesses are usually quite busy, it's best to do this well in advance. Experts can be expensive, but sometimes they can be the deciding factor for a jury.

One of the most important things we do as we prepare for trial is to also prepare our client. The thought of a trial is scary for anyone. It is our job to not only defend our clients, but also make sure that they are aware of what is going on, why it is going on, and what is likely to come next.

For example, a defendant has an absolute right to testify at their trial. They also have an absolute right not to testify. It is our job to make them aware of all the benefits and risks of testifying for and/or against themself.

One of the next things we do with trial preparation is to start to interview any witnesses that we thought we might be using at trial. We would go through the state's witness list and try to anticipate which witnesses the state might actually call. A common practice by the state is to give you a list of 20+ potential witnesses they may call, when they only intend to call three or four of those 20+. Typically, in a drug case, the state will have an analyst testify about the drugs in question and the testing that was done to determine what the substance was. Generally, we would go through that expert's curriculum vitae to make sure that they are properly trained and certified, we may question the process used, the chain of custody for the substance in question, the temperature at which it was stored, many different factors may be important, depending upon our defensive issues at trial.

In Texas, our trial system is bifurcated, meaning we have two stages. The first stage is to determine guilt or innocence. If the jury or the judge finds the person guilty, then you move on to the next phase which is punishment. If the person is found not guilty, then everything ends there and you don't have to go into the second punishment phase.

Assuming the person is found guilty, you would then move right into punishment directly after the verdict is given. In addition to preparing for trial and deciding our trial strategy, we have to also make a decision about putting together evidence for mitigation, in the event that you are found guilty. We have to be prepared to put on punishment witnesses and seek the best punishment that we can from the judge or jury regardless of how strong we may think our case is or not. All of the punishment evidence must be compiled beforehand. This throws a lot of clients off as we prepare for trial because it makes them think we are expecting them to be found guilty. That is not the case. The reality is that you never know what a jury of 12 people (or 6 people if the charge is a misdemeanor) are going to do. So, no matter what, as a lawyer, you have to be prepared for everything. You wouldn't want your attorney defending you to have prepared nothing in your defense when it comes to what punishment should be assessed.

In preparing for punishment should it get to that point, we compile evidence of good character and other mitigating factors that may be present. Let's say that a client was just found guilty but maybe that client has had a serious and longstanding drug problem for quite some time. Maybe they just need some type of rehabilitation or treatment to address the issue. Presenting this type of evidence at the punishment phase would be helpful for mitigation purposes for any punishment that was to come. In the appropriate situations, we have clients begin treatment early on, so that we can show the Court/Prosecutor/Jury that our client is being proactive in addressing the problem.

Another way we prepare for punishment is to talk to character witnesses who may be able to testify for the defendant in court and speak to the type of person the defendant is. The goal is to humanize the client to the judge and jury so that they may assess the least amount of punishment possible for the crime and specific defendant.

At What Point in My Drug Case Will the Prosecutor Generally Offer a Plea Deal?

A lot of times, the timing as to when we will get a plea offer on a defendant depends on whether they are in jail or not. A person in jail is going to generally take preference over a bonded client and they will likely receive an offer sooner than someone who is out on bond. Whether a person has criminal history or not is also a huge factor as to when or if we receive a plea offer from the state. A person with no criminal history is not on the state's radar as much as someone who does from the state's perspective. This is because the defendant without significant criminal history is not a multiple time offender.

On the flip side of that, a defendant who has a criminal history and is enhanced is going to probably receive an offer much later in the game. The state can be prompted to make an offer. It just depends on the type of case as to whether we do that or not and whether it will benefit our client in the long run.

CHAPTER 4

HOW COMMON IS IT TO ASSUME THERE WILL NEVER BE A CHANCE TO WIN A DRUG CASE IN TEXAS?

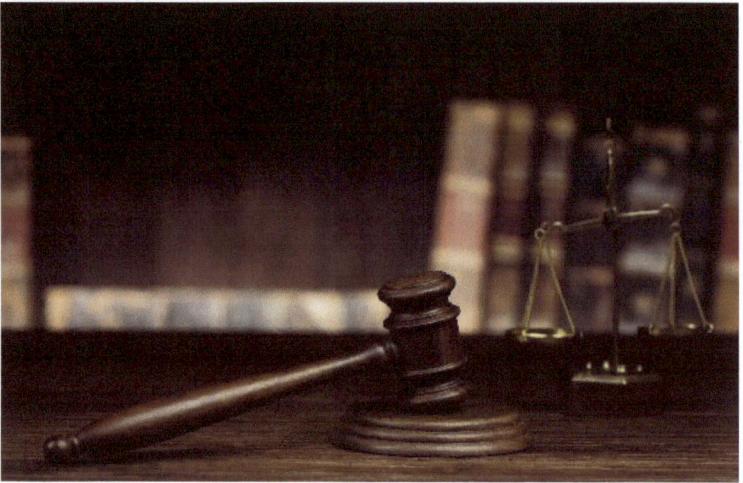

Most clients fall on one of two sides of the spectrum – they are either convinced they are going to lose or convinced that they are going to win. Clients rarely find themselves in the middle of those two ways of thinking. Unfortunately, the issue is that most cases fall into that gray area somewhere in the middle. There may indeed be an issue in a case, but it may not be as fatal to the state's case as we or the client hoped it would be. It is one of our duties as your attorneys to bring you into the loop and make you understand what is going on and how it impacts your case. If you don't fully understand the process, that is what we are here for; once you know the full picture, you can make the best decision about how to move forward with the disposition of your case with us alongside you throughout the process.

At What Point in Drug Cases Do You Generally Get Hired on by the Client/Defendant?

In every case, it is a good idea to hire your attorney early on. It is especially important in drug cases. You need someone representing you who is going to be able to get evidence in your case that can help you. If you hire an attorney later, they may not have the ability to get that evidence. Maybe the evidence has become stale or there is now an inability to get it.

For example, there is a retention period for some (if not most) police departments. After a certain amount of time, evidence cannot be procured if needed for your defense. There may be video evidence available from a non-law enforcement source, area business, ring doorbell, etc. Most videos are recorded over at varying intervals and if you wait too long, that potential evidence may no longer be available to you from non-law enforcement as well.

In addition, there are a lot of side issues that commonly come up with drug cases. A lot of courts impose bond conditions requiring defendants to drug test every thirty days and/or each time they come to court. That is not something you want to do alone in court without representation. Having an attorney present with you during this process will likely mitigate the issues that may arise as result. This doesn't have much to actually do with the crime that the person is charged with. Nonetheless, we are here to help the client every step of the way throughout the entire process.

CHAPTER 5

DEFENSES OFTEN USED IN DRUG POSSESSION CASES

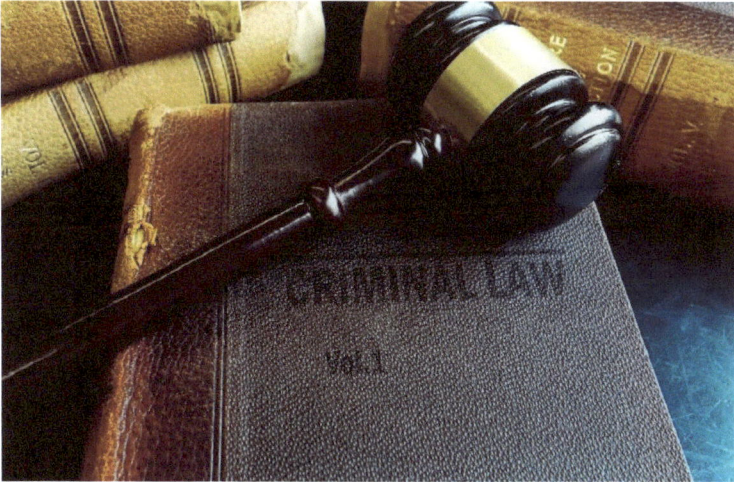

In many possession cases, the client will have a prescription for the drug that they are charged with possessing. It doesn't completely exonerate them or make them not guilty but for the most part, we can a lot of the time get a dismissal in these cases. Another very common defense would be what we refer to as a bad stop, a bad search, or a bad seizure, meaning a Fourth Amendment violation. If we have a constitutional violation present, then everything that follows is thrown out. It is not allowed to be used as evidence against that defendant if it was obtained in violation of your constitutional rights.

Another defense is that the state charged the defendant with the wrong controlled substance. For example, someone is charged with cocaine possession and the DPS crime lab confirms that the substance is actually not cocaine. We have seen this issue quite a bit, sometimes to the surprise of our client. We have also had clients tell us in advance that the substance will not be an illicit drug.

On the following page we've included a table of common drugs and the category they fall into from Penalty Group ("PG") 1 through 4 under the Texas Health and Safety Code, specifically Chapter 481 Texas Controlled Substances Act. The specific charge the State accuses the defendant of must be specified correctly into one of the following four penalty groups. The State must elect which category they plan to prosecute the defendant under and there must be proof to substantiate this.

Common PG 1 Drugs	• Cociane • Methamphetamine • Heroin • Flunitrazepam (Rohypnol) • Gamma Hydroxybutyric Acid (GHB)
Common PG 2 (& 2-A) Drugs	• Tetrahydrocannabinols (THC), other than marijuana • Most Amphetamines • Psylocybin (Mushrooms) • Synthetic Cannabinoids (also known as K2 and Spice)
Common PG 3 Drugs	• Alprazolam (Xanax) • Clonazepam (Rivotril) • Diazepam (Valium) • Methylphenidate (Ritalin) • Lorazepam (Ativan)
Common PG 4 Drugs	• Opioids and opiates not listed in PG 1 • Generally prescription medications that contain small doses of narcotics in combination with other drugs, such as Tylenol 3

We also have a legal definition for what possession is and how someone can legally be in possession of a substance. This can be another defense that may present itself in drug possession cases. There must be some element of knowledge incorporated into it and that is sometimes difficult for the state to prove. How do you get into someone's mind and prove that they knew the drug was there? We utilize that that a lot in our cases. They have to prove beyond a reasonable doubt that someone knew about something, unless there are other circumstances to corroborate it.

What Is the Most Important Information That I Should Share with My Attorney?

The short answer to this is that you should share everything with your attorney. Holding information back from your lawyer who is defending you is never a good idea.

Specifically, here are some examples of important things that you must communicate with your attorney. Failing to do so will negatively impact you and your case.

- Once the police make the arrest, they have little to no involvement in the case. The District Attorney takes over at that point. However, the police are very often trying to continue communication with the defendant to get more information on their case or on another case. If a police officer was to reach out to you, you need to immediately tell your attorney.

- If your case falls into a court that randomly drug tests you or tests you at your court settings, if you have reason to believe your drug/alcohol test will be dirty, you need to let us know. We need adequate time to prepare for what is to come and protect or shield you from potential consequences of failing a drug/alcohol test.

- Another thing we need to know about immediately would be a new arrest, whether in the same county or anywhere else, even if it is completely unrelated. It is always relevant and important for us to know when you get arrested on a new case while you're on bond for another case.

Is It Possible for My Attorney to Work with the Prosecutor to Have My Charges Reduced to a Lesser Offense?

There are usually plenty of opportunities to have charges dismissed or reduced based on the specific type of case and if the attorney knows what they are doing in handling your case. A very common occurrence is that a suspected substance is found on an accused person and weighed by the officer in whatever container it was found in, making the total weight of the substance much heavier than the actual controlled substance itself is. However, the way our system works, you can only be charged with the amount of the actual substance. Oftentimes, we will have someone charged with more than a gram of a particular substance but then when it is sent to the laboratory and measured, it will come back as less than a gram. These are times when we see charges being reduced frequently. An entire felony level can be reduced, which is substantial when you are talking about punishment.

Should Someone Start Counseling or a Drug Rehabilitation Program While Their Drug Related Case Is Pending?

If someone has a substance abuse or alcohol issue that they need help with, professional help should not be avoided. If you need help, you should seek treatment. However, oftentimes the families of defendants will push drug rehabilitation because they believe that it will make the case go away since the defendant sought help for the issue. The thought process is that this will make everyone involved in the process satisfied and not as willing to punish the person for the crime they are charged with. More often than not though, it does not have a significant impact on the resolution of the case. The better way to approach something like that would be to talk to your attorney first so they can get your court settings addressed with the court so you do not get in trouble for not being there assuming you are in a facility you cannot leave.

There is definitely an ability for us to talk to the judge and the prosecutor to potentially set a person up to go to a facility to seek treatment while the case is pending. The issue that we see is when people go to treatment and they don't think about their court settings. You cannot disregard your court dates without permission from the judge. Your lawyer should be the one to help you with issues such as this. Another important aspect here is that typically rehab only works if the person is committed to the program and getting help, we have seen over and over families trying to force rehab on their loved ones, and when forced, it rarely produces success.

CHAPTER 6

WHY IS IT IMPORTANT TO RETAIN AN EXPERIENCED ATTORNEY TO FIGHT DRUG CHARGES?

Drug cases often come down to legal technicalities that a person who doesn't have legal experience would never even believe could get you out of a case. For example, if you are pulled over for speeding and you are found with kilos upon kilos of a drug, if you can prove that you actually weren't speeding, then in theory you cannot be prosecuted for that drug crime. You only know these things after you are taught them by going through time and time again defending drug cases. It is important to have someone who knows what they are doing beside you because you could miss those things and if you do, you could miss an opportunity to potentially have your case dismissed or evidence suppressed.

If you just roll over and take a plea, you could end up in a situation where if it happens again, you are going to be prosecuted a lot more heavily and your punishment range goes up. Once you have a spot on your record, the police know and they do not forget. It is a decision that is going to have lasting effects.

What Is Your Experience and Approach in Defending Clients and Impact Their Outcome?

Mark has over 20 years of experience in defending drug crimes. He knows how to very quickly analyze a case and he knows which officers to watch for regarding certain behaviors they may have exhibited in the past. He knows that, within our jurisdiction, certain judges have particular feelings about one type of drug over another. The experience he has is invaluable. He's read thousands and thousands of police reports and looked at hundreds of thousands of hours of videos of searches and seizures. There is nothing he could do to replace time and experience. It becomes like a second language.

Jessica was a prosecutor in Galveston County before she became a defense attorney. With cases that were assigned to her, when certain defense attorneys would walk into the courtroom representing defendants, based on the caliber of attorney they had, the case was treated differently. The reality is that clients are treated differently by the system based on who they have representing them. For example, when she was still a prosecutor, she went up against Mark a few times in cases and each time she knew she had her work cut out for her. Whether it was a case she believed was strong or weak, she knew Mark was the type of defense attorney who would make her earn that conviction and that stands true to this day.

INDEX

NOTES

www.ingramcontent.com/pod-product-compliance
Lightning Source LLC
Chambersburg PA
CBHW041721200326
41521CB00004B/167